MULLION COVE HOTEL

'The Gem of the Cornish Coast'

High on the cliffs overlooking the working harbour

❋ ❋ ❋

Stunning coastal views and superb food and wines

❋ ❋ ❋

Fresl

Cove Ba

Enjoy
Cove
(r

G000297474

**Local steaks, fresh fish and shellfish, often brought
up from the Cove, a speciality**

AA
★★★
Hotel

Mullion, South Cornwall, TR12 7EP
Telephone: 01326 240328 Fax 01326 240998
Email: mullion.cove@btinternet.com
Web: http://www.mullioncove.com

*(1) Flint and chert from Loe Bar
(2) Schist from Porthoustock (3) Gabbro from
Porthoustock (4) Banded gabbro from
Porthoustock (5) Pink granite from Kennack
Sands (6) Green serpentine from Kennack
Sands (7) Red serpentine from Kynance Cove
(8) Troutstone from Coverack (9) Quartz*

The Lizard Peninsula

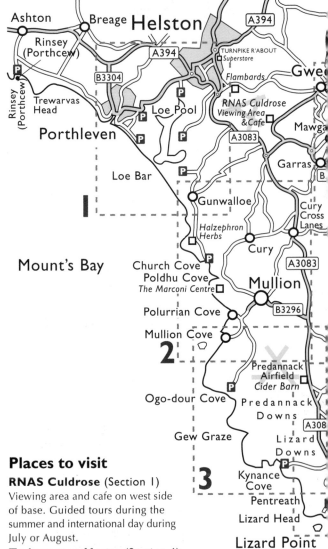

Places to visit

RNAS Culdrose (Section 1)
Viewing area and cafe on west side of base. Guided tours during the summer and international day during July or August.

Trelowarren House (Section 6)
Lizard Countryside Centre, Cornwall Craft Association Gallery, bistro & pottery. Woodland walks during the season.

Lizard Countryside Centre
At Trelowarren House - the best introduction to the geology, archaeology and wildlife of the Lizard Peninsula & the perfect way to get your bearings at the start of your visit.

Lizard Point (Section 4) [T1]
The most southerly point in the UK. Wonderful in gales as the waves break over the Man O'War reef. Concrete road leads to the derelict lifeboat house in Polpeor Cove.

Kynance Cove (Section 3) [T3]
Famous beauty spot. Reached by road from the A3083 on Lizard Downs or by footpath from Lizard Village. Best visited at low water when the islands become accessible. Likely to be busy in the summer school holidays. Cafe above cove.

Goonhilly Earth Satellite Station (Section 6) [T2]
State-of-the-art satellite station in wonderful contrast with the primitive, bleak wildness of Goonhilly Downs. Handles millions of phone calls a year. Visitor centre, children's adventure playground, surf the Internet.

Flambards Theme Park, Helston (Section 1) [T1]
The best funfair in Cornwall with roller coaster ride and static displays of helicopters and aircraft from the adjacent naval air base. Very busy in school holidays especially on overcast days. Reduced entry fee in the afternoon.

Roskilly's Ice Cream (Section 5)

Ice cream to die for - made on the farm with milk from their own cows. Watch milking every afternoon. Evening barbecues. Wildlife trail follows the valley down to Godrevy Cove, once the home to the notorious footpads of the Long Meadow Gang.

Trebah & Glendurgan Gardens (Section 7)
Famous sub tropical gardens on the north bank of the Helford. Take the pedestrian ferry from Helford Village. Cafes and plant sales. Trebah Garden is particularly child centered.

National Seal Sanctuary, Gweek (Section 6)
Hospital for hurt and injured seals and seal pups. Most are returned to the wild on their recovery. Permanent residents include sealions. Best time to visit is feeding time.

Wreck Diving & Boat Trips
Diving tuition for novices at Porthkerris Cove. Dive on wrecks on the Manacles Reef. Boat trips leave from Cadgwith & Mullion in the summer to view the coast, watch seals & for fishing trips.

Boat hire & sailing tuition
From St Anthony on Carne Creek at the mouth of the Helford river - telephone (01326) 231357 and from Helford Passage - telephone (01326) 250770.

Helston Flora Day
Held every year on 8th of May except when that falls on a Sunday or Monday, in which case it is held on the preceding Saturday. The town is decorated with greenery and flowers and the population dance through the town, in and out of the houses.

Pubs with a sea view
Pubs where you can sit out with a view over the ocean.
Ship Inn, Porthleven; *Halzephron Inn*, Gunwalloe; *Cove Hotel*, Cadgwith (Cornish songs on a Friday night); *Paris Hotel*, Coverack; *Five Pilchards*, Porthallow; *Shipwrights Arms*, Helford Village; *Ferry Boat Inn*, Helford Passage (via ferry from Helford Village).

Gazetteer
Beach Guide

Pentreath Beach

Most of the good beaches on the Lizard such as Gunwalloe, Poldhu, Polurrian and Kynance are on the west coast facing over Mount's Bay. They have golden sand and are of course always very popular. The beaches on the more sheltered east coast tend to be more pebbly but they can be gloriously empty such as Godrevy beach near St Keverne. The great exception to this rule is the wonderful beach at Kennack Sands. Best beaches for drama - Rinsey or Mullion Cove; for tranquillity - Grebe beach on the north bank of the Helford.

Rinsey Cove (Porthcew)
This lovely little beach is on the very edge of the Lizard - 4km northwest of Porthleven below an old tin mine. 10 minute walk down cliff from National Trust car park at Rinsey. Take turning off A394 (Helston-Penzance road) at Ashton and follow signs to Rinsey or take the minor road that winds up past the Ship Inn in Porthleven. Slightly awkward climb over rocks down onto beach. Sand only at low water although people swim off the rocks at high water. No facilities. Very highly recommended.

Porthleven - Eastern Beach (Section 1)
Sandy beach just outside the harbour wall. Swimming dangerous at low tide or in rough conditions. All facilities in Porthleven.

Loe Bar (Section 1)
Dangerous shelving beach with fast offshore currents. Avoid walking too close to the sea edge as freak waves occur here even on otherwise calm days. A number of lives have been lost here in recent years as unwary visitors have been swamped by waves and then dragged back into the sea. It is a great place to walk but nobody in their right mind ever swims here.

Gunwalloe - Church Cove (Section 2)
Perfect family beach. Plenty of sand even at high water with a stream for small children to play in. Small cafe sells refreshments and pasties. Search for Spanish treasure from a wrecked ship at Dollar Cove. Large National Trust car park above the beach.

Poldhu Cove (Section 2)
Popular, large sandy beach with cafe & large car park. Good cliff walks on either side of the cove.

Polurrian Cove (Section 2)
Popular, large sandy beach. Nearest parking is in Mullion Village about 10 minutes walk from beach.

Mullion Cove (Section 2/3)
Wide expanse of sand only exposed a low tide. Accessible via tunnel from Mullion Cove harbour. Perfect for cricket & football and perfectly set against high cliffs of dark serpentine. Car park, cafe & toilets 5 minutes above Mullion Cove harbour.

Beach patrolled by lifeguard   Dogs allowed all year. Other beaches have dog ban Easter-Oct

Kynance Cove (Section 3) 🦽 T3 - see photo page 24.
Really a beach for exploring rather than swimming. Numerous islands & wonderful caves with polished walls of serpentine. Be aware of the tide as one can easily become stranded. Park in National Trust car park 10 minutes walk above the cove. Refreshments and toilets at car park, cafe at cove. Car park often becomes full early in the day during school summer holidays and bank holidays.

Pentreath Beach (Section 3/4) 🐕
Isolated, uncrowded sand and pebble beach below cliffs. Sand only at low water. Park at National Trust car park above Kynance and then 1km walk to beach or at Lizard village car park and walk across the downs. No facilities. See photo left.

Housel Cove (Section 4) - see photo on front cover. 🦽
Small beach at foot of cliffs. Moderately difficult decent. Housel Bay Hotel above cove provides bar snacks and meals. Park at car park above Lizard Point then 1km walk along cliff path.

Cadgwith Cove (Section 4)(🐕 eastern cove)
Small beach covered at high water. Pub, toilet and shops above beach. Large Car Park 5 minutes walk above Cadgwith Cove

Kennack Sands (Section 4) ▭ 🦽 (🐕 eastern beach)
Wonderful family beach with golden sand, streams and rock pools. Large car park, cafe, shop & toilets.

Coverack (Section 5) 🐕 T3
Good beach for playing football. Gentle walk to Lowland Point. All facilities in Coverack.

Leggan & Godrevy Cove (Section 5) 🐕
Wonderfully deserted pebbly beaches. Extremely limited roadside parking at Rosenithon or park above Polcries Cove. No facilities.

Porthoustock Cove (Section 5) 🐕
Pebbly beach sandwiched between quarries. Mostly used by divers exploring the wrecks surrounding The Manacles.

Porthallow Cove (Section 5/7) 🐕
Pebbly beach easily accessible from large beach car park. Five Pilchards pub, cafes & other facilities nearby.

Gillan Beach (Section 7) 🐕
Small sandy cove much used by yachts. Quiet, no facilities.

Bosahan Cove (Section 7)
The first of three tiny hidden sandy beaches on the coast path between St Anthony and Helford Village. Park at St Anthony, no facilities, may lose sun in late afternoon. No dogs on coast path.

Passage Cove (Section 7) 🦽
Small sandy beach on north side of Helford River. Good for taking children as getting there from the Lizard side involves taking the pedestrian ferry from Helford Village (check ferry times on 01326 250770). Parents can sit and sip cocktails in the Ferry Boat Inn and still be able to supervise children on the beach. Short walk east to the gardens of Trebah and Glendurgan.

Grebe Beach (Section 7) 🦽 T4
One of the best small beaches in Cornwall and a bit of a secret - 10 minutes walk from Helford Passage. National Trust car park at top of hill above beach. No facilities.

BUS SERVICES TRURONIAN OPERATE ON THE LIZARD

T1	**Service T1** Perranporth - St Agnes - Truro - Helston - Mullion - The Lizard with EASY ACCESS BUSES (Mondays to Saturdays & Sundays in the summer) serving Flambards Theme Park
T2	**Service T2** Helston - Coverack & St Keverne with connections to Truro (Mondays to Saturdays) serving Goonhilly Earth Satellite Station
T3	**Service T3 - The Lizard Rambler** Helston - Mawgan - St Martin - Helford Village - Manaccan - Porthallow- St Keverne-Tregellast Barton- Coverack- Ruan Minor - Kynance Cove (Mon-Sat & Sun in the summer) serving Roskilly's
T4	**Service T4** Helston to Falmouth (Mondays to Saturdays & Sundays in the summer) serving Gweek, Trebah/Glendurgan Gardens & Helford Passage

For information tel. Truronian Buses (01872) 273453

🦽 *Good family beach - these beaches usually offer large nearby car parks with cafe and toilets*

Introduction

The Lizard peninsula has a distinctive and exotic quality that makes it feel quite different to other parts of Cornwall. This is partly because the Lizard is practically an island. The only land link with the rest of Cornwall is the thin spine that forms the watershed between the wooded valleys of the Helford river that flow east into Falmouth Bay, and the Carnminowe stream that flows west to Loe Pool and into Mount's Bay. Having passed along this spine you find yourself not in the characteristic Cornish landscape of rolling slate hills and craggy granite uplands, but in a landscape where the usual geology has been substituted by a medley of strange rocks. It is these rocks that dictate the unusual character of the Lizard.

In this remote part of Cornwall Mother Nature has reluctantly given up rocks that are rarely exposed at the surface of the earth and properly make up the core of our planet. At the centre of the peninsula is a plateau of uncultivated ancient heath almost untouched by man. This bleak area which comprises Goonhilly, Predannack and Lizard Downs corresponds with the outcrop of a rock called serpentine. This rock forms the huge volume of the mantle below the thin (7km) outer crust of the earth. Very occasionally it is torn from the mantle and exposed at the surface.

The serpentine forms a waterlogged and unwilling clay soil with few nutrients and this is why it is left uncultivated. However, the rocks that surround the serpentine such as schist and gabbro form unusually deep and fertile soils that will nourish almost any seed a farmer cares to scatter. The division between these rocks and the serpentine is often very clear and sharp. The vegetation may completely change within a few metres from lush pasture to windblown heath and this tends to reinforce the sense of strangeness that one sometimes feels on the Lizard.

Geology

The rocks of the Lizard are thought to represent types usually found in a vertical sequence in the earth's oceanic crust - the portion of the earth that reaches down about seven kilometres from the sea bed to the mantle - the outer part of the earth's core. This typical sequence of rocks is called an *ophiolite* and is occasionally torn from the mantle and thrust onto the surface by huge and prolonged earth movements. The different rocks of the ophiolite come from the same source - the mantle, but they become altered in their passage to the surface. The type of rock they change into depends on varying factors such as how rapidly they cool and what contact they have with other chemicals on their passage from the mantle. For instance, molten rock from the mantle erupted onto the sea floor is very rapidly chilled and its chemical composition is altered as it comes into contact with sea water. The typical type of rock formed at the sea bed is a hard *basalt* or *pillow lava*. Mullion Island is composed of pillow lava. Molten magma that does not make it to the surface will cool much more slowly to form large crystalline rocks such as *gabbro*. The serpentine rock which forms over half the area of the Lizard, is rarely seen at the surface because it constitutes the source rock in the mantle and it can only reach the surface in its unaltered state, if it has already solidified many kilometres underground and is then physically ripped from there by earth movements.

From a geological perspective the surface of the earth is in constant motion. The rocks of the mantle behave in a semi-fluid way distributing heat from the hot, molten core of the earth to the cooler, surface of the planet. A movement is set up within the mantle where hot, and therefore less dense rock rises, and cooler, denser rock sinks. This form of heat distribution is called a *convection cell* and is active throughout the universe at every level. In our atmosphere it is this mechanism that drives the weather as warm air from the equator is distributed to the colder poles. It is the same mechanism that cools a cup of tea. As a result of this fluid movement the solid surface crust of the earth is broken up into huge crustal plates floating above the mantle. The continents which are formed of less dense sedimentary and igneous rocks are then propelled around the surface of the earth by the movement of the convection cells. This geological process, which acts over many millions of years is called *continental drift*. In our lives we experience this motion of the continents in as earthquakes when the earth's crust fractures and moves, sometimes by as much as two or three metres at a time.

Since the formation of our planet about 4.5 billion years ago the shape of the crustal plates has changed as the fluid convection cells within the planet change direction. The plates are constantly jostling with one another, sometimes smashing into each other to form mountain ranges and single super-continents, and sometimes sliding past each other as at the San Andreas fault in California. Plates will break apart into smaller sections as convection cells well up beneath them. In this way rocks formed in the southern hemisphere can be transported by continental drift to the northern hemisphere. Analysis of the rocks of Cornwall has shown some were formed at a position near the equator and have since been driven north by continental drift. The enormous pressures and strains of movement can also be expressed in the rocks themselves - sedimentary rocks laid down as horizontal layers can be squeezed into tight vertical folds in a sort of ultra slow motion crash - this can be seen in the folded slates at Jangye-ryn beach near Gunwalloe.

The Lizard appears to lie in the collision zone between

The flat plateau of Goonhilly Downs was once an ancient seabed

two ancient continental plates - the Normannian Plate to the south and the Laurasian Plate to the north. They became fused together about 375 million years ago. The oceanic crust that originally divided them was mostly overridden but a portion of the crust caught in this collision seems to have become thrust up to the surface of the earth. This is the sequence of rocks that make up the larger part of the Lizard. The schist rocks that surround the ophiolite represent silt and sediment laid down on the sea floor but which have been altered by the intense pressures of the earth movements which brought the ophiolite to the surface. Rocks of the southern Normannian plate are represented by the rocks of the Man O'War reef off Lizard Point. They are very similar to rocks found in Normandy and Brittany and therefore thought to be part of the same plate and are possibly as much as 600 million years old. The original rocks of the Laurasian plate are not visible but the slates that make up the northern boundary of the Lizard are thought to be formed at least in part from sediment resulting from the erosion of the Laurasian mountains.

The Meneage breccia is a mile wide band of debris that makes up over half of the northern boundary of the Lizard. It is composed of a mush of different rock types some of which are not known to outcrop locally but are assumed to be remnants accumulated in front of the Normannian plate as it pushed north. They contain large rafts of quartzite a rock similar in age to the rocks of the Man O'War reef.

Landscape

One of the lovely things about exploring the coves and downs of the Lizard is the way in which the relationship between the bedrock and the landscape is so clearly visible. The sea will exploit and erode any junction between different rocks to form a cove and on the Lizard this helpfully marks the junction between most of the rock types. At Polurrian you find a boundary between the slates of Cornwall and the schists of the Lizard; at Mullion Cove the boundary between the schists and the

Rocks of the Lizard

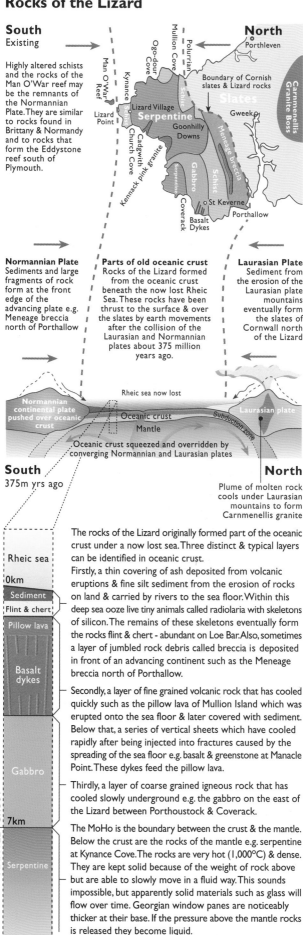

South
Existing

Highly altered schists and the rocks of the Man O'War reef may be the remnants of the Normannian Plate. They are similar to rocks found in Brittany & Normandy and to rocks that form the Eddystone reef south of Plymouth.

North

Porthleven
Mullion Cove
Polurrian
Ogo-dour Cove
Man O'War Reef
Kynance
Schist
Boundary of Cornish slates & Lizard rocks
Carnmenellis Granite Boss
Slates
Gweek
Lizard Village
Serpentine
Lizard Point
Goonhilly Downs
Cadgwith
Church Cove
Kennack pink granite
Gabbro
Serpentine
Schist
Meneage breccia
St Keverne
Coverack
Basalt Dykes
Porthallow

Normannian Plate
Sediments and large fragments of rock form at the front edge of the advancing plate e.g. Meneage breccia north of Porthallow

Parts of old oceanic crust
Rocks of the Lizard formed from the oceanic crust beneath the now lost Rheic Sea. These rocks have been thrust to the surface & over the slates by earth movements after the collision of the Laurasian and Normannian plates about 375 million years ago.

Laurasian Plate
Sediment from the erosion of the Laurasian plate mountains eventually form the slates of Cornwall north of the Lizard

Rheic sea now lost

Normannian continental plate pushed over oceanic crust
Oceanic crust
Mantle
Laurasian plate
Subduction zone

Oceanic crust squeezed and overridden by converging Normannian and Laurasian plates

South
375m yrs ago

North
Plume of molten rock cools under Laurasian mountains to form Carnmenellis granite

Rheic sea
0km
Sediment
Flint & chert
Pillow lava
Basalt dykes
Gabbro
7km
Serpentine
MANTLE | CRUST

The rocks of the Lizard originally formed part of the oceanic crust under a now lost sea. Three distinct & typical layers can be identified in oceanic crust.

Firstly, a thin covering of ash deposited from volcanic eruptions & fine silt sediment from the erosion of rocks on land & carried by rivers to the sea floor. Within this deep sea ooze live tiny animals called radiolaria with skeletons of silicon. The remains of these skeletons eventually form the rocks flint & chert - abundant on Loe Bar. Also, sometimes a layer of jumbled rock debris called breccia is deposited in front of an advancing continent such as the Meneage breccia north of Porthallow.

Secondly, a layer of fine grained volcanic rock that has cooled quickly such as the pillow lava of Mullion Island which was erupted onto the sea floor & later covered with sediment. Below that, a series of vertical sheets which have cooled rapidly after being injected into fractures caused by the spreading of the sea floor e.g. basalt & greenstone at Manacle Point. These dykes feed the pillow lava.

Thirdly, a layer of coarse grained igneous rock that has cooled slowly underground e.g. the gabbro on the east of the Lizard between Porthoustock & Coverack.

The MoHo is the boundary between the crust & the mantle. Below the crust are the rocks of the mantle e.g. serpentine at Kynance Cove. The rocks are very hot (1,000°C) & dense. They are kept solid because of the weight of rock above but are able to slowly move in a fluid way. This sounds impossible, but apparently solid materials such as glass will flow over time. Georgian window panes are noticeably thicker at their base. If the pressure above the mantle rocks is released they become liquid.

serpentine; at Coverack the boundary between the serpentine and gabbro and so on around the coastline.

Each rock forms a characteristic coastal scenery. The number and variety of rocks found on the Lizard make the coastline the most interesting in Cornwall. The Serpentine forms the highest cliffs because it is the most resistant rock having been forged in the centre of the earth. Hence it forms the dark emerald cliffs south of Mullion Cove and the 90 metre high cliffs of Vellan Head. The slates, weakened by intense deformation, form an indented coast of low cliffs like those at Gunwalloe and the rolling landscape of The Meneage. Faults or cracks within any type of rock are attacked and eroded by the sea to form deep caves. These caves often become homes for seals, particularly on the west coast beyond Lizard Head. Where the roofs of the caves become unstable they can collapse to form hollows and holes such as the Devil's Frying Pan south of Cadgwith, and The Lion's Den near Lizard Point.

Inland, the boundaries between the rocks are less obvious as the whole peninsula was planed flat when the rocks were part of an ancient seabed 200 million years ago. Subsequent erosion by wind and rain has eroded valleys in the rocks surrounding the serpentine. Where pink granite replaces the serpentine, it is the weaker granite that has been eroded to form the few coves and valleys in the south of the Lizard at Cadgwith, Poltesco and Kennack Sands. The serpentine itself is so tough, it is virtually the same surface that formed the sea bed so many millions of years ago. This accounts for the table top flatness of Goonhilly and Lizard Downs. We know the Lizard was once submerged because gravels and typical seabed deposits still exist on top of the serpentine at Crousa Down 100 metres above the present sea level. These have been extensively quarried by man. It is this flat surface that attracted the air force to build the airfield at Predannack and the wide, uninterrupted sky that attracted British Telecom to build Goonhilly Earth Satellite Station.

Plants, Animals and People

The Lizard has a typical maritime climate, characterised by wet mild winters and dry summers. As a result of this mild climate many sub tropical plants are able to grow here that would not survive further north in Britain. The Helford River has two internationally famous gardens on its north bank - the National Trust garden at Glendurgan and the garden at Trebah. The mildness of the climate allows crops to mature early with many plants blooming at Christmas. It is not simply the southerly latitude of the Lizard that makes the climate so mild. The warming effect of the sea that surrounds the peninsula has an even greater influence. The particular mechanism involved is the Gulf Stream, a sea current that distributes warm water from the equator to the western coasts of Europe. This means that sea temperatures stay within a relatively warm and narrow range throughout the whole year. The beneficial stabilising effect of the Gulf Stream on the climate can be gauged from the fact that Newfoundland lies on a similar latitude to Cornwall, about 50° north of the equator, yet winter temperatures in Newfoundland barely rise above freezing. On the Lizard frosts are rare.

The wild plants of the Lizard are more typical of species found on the Atlantic coasts of Spain and Portugal and it has been suggested that they may be a survival of plants that grew on the original Normannian continent that 'crashed' into Cornwall 375 million years ago. The majority of the wild areas of the Lizard are on the serpentine rock because it only produces poor soils for agriculture. The serpentine supports an unusual community of plants and animals. It is very poorly drained and tends to form permanent and semi-permanent standing pools of water. This creates a perfect environment for reptiles and amphibians and much of the downs and cliffs are of national importance in this regard. Some species have adapted to exploit the temporary pools on the downs. Frogs and toads will often spawn before Christmas to allow their young to grow before the ponds dry out in early summer. Britain's only venomous snake, the adder thrives on the heath and they can often be seen basking in the sun near pools.

The mineral composition of serpentine includes large amounts of magnesium from one of the constituent minerals - olivine. The magnesium rich soil supports a community of plants more often found on bedrocks such as chalk, also rich in magnesium. Orchids thrive on the cliffs at above Mullion and Predannack. The National Trust graze hardy Soay sheep and Shetland ponies on the cliffs to keep down the bracken and gorse that would otherwise strangle the delicate orchids. They perform the job once done by indigenous wild ponies called Goonhillies, now unfortunately extinct.

The seas and reefs around the Lizard are also rich in wildlife. Grey seals breed in the deep caves west of Lizard Head. They spend most of their lives at sea but come inshore to moult and breed. September and October are the main breeding months. The pups are born in deep and secluded sea caves. The cows are able to give an exceptionally rich milk that allows the pups to gain nine kilos in the first week after birth. The main danger to the pups is a storm because even the deepest cave is not above the highest storm tides. After three weeks the pup is abruptly deserted by its mother and over the next two weeks it lives off its fat whilst its sea coat grows. At this time the cows will mate again as there are a convenient number of bulls to choose from,

Plants of the Downs

Cornish Heath (left)
The characteristic
shrub of the downs.
Found only on the
Lizard.

Purple Tufted Vetch
(right)

Spring Sandwort (left)
Has a strong
toleration of the
metals present in
serpentine. They
usually interfer with
plant metabalism.

Burnet Rose (right)

Hemp Agrimony (left)
A common plant of
damp waterlogged
areas particularly
roadside ditches.

Common Centaury
(right). Frequent on
the poor, stony soils
of the coast

Purple Orchid (left).
Often found on road
verges where its dust
like seeds are carried
in the slip streams of
cars.

Self Heal (right)

Heath Spotted Orchid
(left). Found on the
acidic wind blown
soils of the downs.

Dropwort (right)

Betony (left)

Black Bog Rush
(right)

The numerous pools and ponds of the Lizard heaths and downs are particularly suited to insects and reptiles.

but the fertilised egg will be not develop until spring. The bulls are more conspicuous than the cows because of their darker coats and larger size. They look a bit like sumo wrestlers because of the luxurious rolls of fat around their necks. The males will grow up to 2.5 metres long and live up to about 25 years. The females grow up to 1.8 metres long and live for up to 35 years. The seals will return to the caves in January and February to moult and allow their new sea coats to grow. Seals are easiest to spot between Lizard Point and Kynance and a smaller number breed west of Porthleven. Boats from Mullion make special trips to watch the seals.

Dolphins are also seen from the cliffs usually in pods of 30 or 40 individuals following shoals of mackerel and mullet. They make the task of swimming look less like a chore and seem more like a party. The sight of a pod of dolphins will undoubtedly make your day. There is no single place where you are guaranteed to see dolphins and the frequency of sightings can vary tremendously from year to year, but it is surprising what you can see from the cliffs if one simply stops, sits down and waits.

Another large and impressive animal regularly sighted from the cliffs in summer is the basking shark, easily identified by their twin black fins and their lugubrious style of swimming. An adult will grow up to 15 metres long and often come in very close to the cliffs trawling the inshore waters for plankton released from barnacles, mussels and other crustaceans. Basking sharks are extremely docile - they spend most of their lives in solitude but in 1998 there was a large and unusual gathering of over 100 off Lizard Point.

The arrival of people on the Lizard is a comparatively recent event in the history of the peninsula. The first people we can say definitely lived here were the *Mesolithic Stone Age* people (7,000-4,000BC). We think they lived nomadically, gathering food from the wild and hunting wild animals, probably similar in to way in which the native America Indians of the 19th century lived. We know of their existence from the discovery of concentrations of flint and chert arrow heads that litter their temporary camps. Croft Pascoe Pool, just south of Traboe Cross is thought to have been a summer camp site. It was during the later Neolithic Stone Age period that these people acquired the skills of agriculture. Neolithic pottery has been found in Crane Carrick Crags near Lowland Point suggesting the rocks may have had some ritual or religious significance. We know that even in the Neolithic period there was a sophisticated trade and exchange of goods on a regional level. Pottery found throughout Cornwall is often found to be composed of clay from the gabbro rock exposed between Porthoustock, Coverack and Kennack Sands. Some pots containing this clay have been found as far away as Brittany. The same rocks are still valued today, but now they are worked for road stone to surface Cornwall's roads.

It was only in the late Neolithic and early Bronze Age (2,500-700BC) that permanent settlements and farming became really established on the Lizard. The area around St Keverne was probably first cultivated at this time and some of the existing stone field boundaries may date from this period. Even today, this area retains many hedges having escaped the worst excesses of hedge clearance in this century. This gives the area much of its outstanding beauty as the hedges provide a haven for wild plants and animals.

Ever since the economy of the Lizard has been based around the twin activities of farming and fishing. The rich schist and gabbro soils making the Lizard the garden of Cornwall. Diversification has never been more relevant with incomes from farming falling and set to decline further as production subsidies are withdrawn. Environmental management and the financial incentives associated with it, are becoming an important source of income for farmers and this is especially true of the Lizard with its rare habitats. The cultivation of bulbs and cut flowers are also important. The mild climate here gives an advantage over northern areas by bringing blooms on more quickly and therefore gaining a premium price in New Covent Garden flower market in London.

Small fishing communities take advantage of every valley for shelter against the sea and storms but with no harbour big or safe enough to hold large fishing vessels most of the trade is conducted from Newlyn on the other side of Mount's Bay. Boats still work from Porthleven and Coverack, but fishing has declined from the days when millions of pilchards might be caught in one day and pressed in the pilchard palaces at Porthallow, Church Cove and Cadgwith. Today, small boats work the coastal reefs and ledges for crab and lobster.

Section 1.
Loe Bar, Porthleven & Helston

The four kilometres of chert and flint shingle that make up Loe Bar dominate this part of the coast. Waves curl around the southern tip of the Land's End Peninsula and fall on the Bar with great ferocity. There are few greater pleasures than coming down here during a gale and getting buffeted by the winds and watching the waves. This has to be followed by a pub lunch in Porthleven or Helzephron. Loe Pool provides a variety of walks and safe cycling for children and is a popular place to watch migrating birds in Spring and Autumn.

Rinsey & Trewarvas Head

Porthcew Cove is a bit outside of the area covered by this guidebook (see key map) but its such a good little beach I have included it here anyway. You can easily walk to Rinsey from Porthleven (4.25km) or follow the directions in the Beach Guide if you are going by car. The beach is set beneath an abandoned tin mine perched on the side of Rinsey cliff. Walking towards Porthleven are the dramatic cliff side mines of Trewarvas Head rather like the well known mines of the Crowns at Botallack on the Land's End Peninsula.

Loe Bar

The Bar is formed mostly of flint, probably driven onto the coast from an undersea outcrop by the extremely strong currents and waves that occur here. The Bar has grown within historic times to block the small estuary of the River Cober forcing the abandonment of Helston Harbour in the early Medieval period. Merchants and traders in Helston needing a port to import and export goods had to turn to Gweek on the Helford river (section 6). The freshwater expanse of Loe Pool has developed behind the bar and attracts many migrating birds. The area around the pool is very accessible with a popular driveway/cycleway on the western side. A quieter footpath follows the eastern side. Look out for the beautiful yellow horned poppy in that flowers near the outlet on the bar in mid summer.

The ferocity of the sea on this part of the coast has to be seen to be believed. In a severe storm the waves will break onto the town clock tower at Porthleven, completely obscuring it. The unusual height of the waves is probably related to the nature of the seabed in Mount's Bay. The waves seem to pile up to a great height off the bar and hit the land with tremendous force. Many thousands of tons of shingle can moved in a single night changing the level of the bar by as much as two metres. Even on an otherwise calm day there maybe a strong ground sea running which will throw unexpectedly large waves onto the bar. A number of lives have been lost in recent years by people being washed off the outer arm of the pier at Porthleven or dragged from the bar into the sea by freak waves. The best advice is simply to admire the sea from a distance and keep back from the sea edge here.

Porthleven

In contrast to most places in West Cornwall Porthleven is still very much a working harbour. Small boats work the local reefs for lobster and crab and hand line for mackerel. Most of the catch is landed at Newlyn near Penzance but fresh fish is always readily available in the shops, restaurants and pubs that line the harbour. The cannon on the harbourside were salvaged from the wreck of the *Anson* - see over. Craft shops operate from the old sail lofts and warehouses.

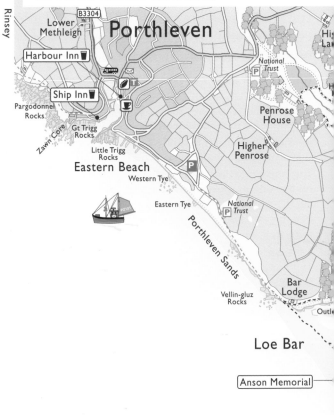

Trewavas Mine

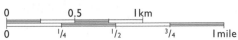

Penzance

Redruth, Truro, Falmouth

P **T**

🏴 **Blue Anchor**

Helston

Boating Lake

A394

P

A394

Porthleven Road

04

P

Penrose Amenity Area

T1,2,3,4

A394

Nansloe Manor Hotel

Helston Cottage Hospital

Lower Nansloe

Nansloe Farm

T1

Flambards Theme Park

Degibna Lane

Recommended Walk

A3083

Royal Naval Air Station Culdrose (HMS Seahawk)

Bird Hide

Nanswidden

e Loe

T1,2,3,4

Degibna

The Lizard

National Trust **P**

Degibna Wood

Higher Pentire

Yellow Horned Poppy

Lower Pentire

Carminowe Mill

Little Nanspian

ninowe Creek

Nanspian

Carminowe

ck

Hendra

National Trust **P**

Chyvarloe

Clies Farm

Burnow Farm

Berepper

Polgrean Farm

Gunwalloe Village

Anhay Farm

Chyanvounder

Gunwalloe Fishing Cove

🏴 **Halzephron Inn**

Trenoweth Farm

Baulk Head

Park Bean Cliff

Park Bean Cove

Fabey's Hole

Herb Farm

Halzephron Cove

Hingey Farm

Toll

Gunwalloe Beach (Church Cove)

Helston

Although Helston is strictly speaking outside the area of the Lizard it has always been intimately linked with the peninsula. It is the nearest large town and has a wider range of facilities than can be found in Mullion or at Lizard village. One of the best facilities available to the visitor is the *Blue Anchor* in Coinagehall Street. It brews its own beer - the famous spingo, reputedly only sold in half pint measures to strangers lest it leave them speechless and trembling with its potency. The town retains the charm of an old county market town. The cattle market still sits at the bottom of the town. The Folk Museum is one of the best in the county and has an intimate atmosphere that brings the local history alive. Old horse drawn fire engines and carts are parked as if they might be called into use at any moment. There are displays of mining artifacts, a huge timber cider press and archaeological finds from the Lizard.

The town sits on the River Cober which flows from the granite high ground to the north east into Loe Pool. Helston adopted Gweek on the Helford river as its port of export when the Cober became blocked by the formation of Loe Bar. Gweek became the port of export for tin won from the moorland steams and Wendron mines after it had been assayed in Helston in the Coinage Hall. It was this trade that made the town so prosperous and financed the fine Georgian buildings.

Helston Flora Day

For many people in Helston Flora Day is the highlight of the year. Many Helstonians travel back from up country especially to take part in the elegant dances. The locals dance the furry dance behind the town band passing through houses and shops in this ancient celebration of Spring. The town becomes very crowded so it is wise to arrive early. All the dances start from the Guildhall. The first dance starts at 7am, followed by the children's dance at 10am, the main dance is at midday and the final dance at 5pm. Don't miss the Hal-an-Tow Dance which starts at about 8am from the Guildhall. The procession stops around the town to enact a ritual fight between St George, a dragon, the devil and some Spanish sailors. A memory of the threat of invasion by the Spanish Armada.

Culdrose Naval Air Station

Culdrose is one of the largest helicopter bases in Europe and is home to 771 Search & Rescue Squadron. They patrol this part of the Cornish coast and have assisted in numerous lifesaving rescues, plucking people off sinking boats and rescuing visitors cut off by the tide. Occasionally, the squadron transport expectant mothers from the Isles of Scilly to the maternity hospital in Truro and recently a baby was actually delivered in one of their helicopters. There is a public viewing enclosure and cafe on the Gweek Road from Helston and tours of the base are organised from here. A collection of helicopters and other aircraft that have been stationed at Culdrose over the last thirty years are on permanent display at the adjacent Flambards Theme Park. An international air day is held each year in July or August.

The Tripolitania wrecked on Loe Bar, Boxing Day 1912.

Loe Bar & The Anson Memorial

In 1807 the Royal Navy frigate *HMS Anson* was driven onto Loe Bar by south westerly gales. She had run for cover into Mount's Bay and let out her anchor in the hope of riding out the storm. Her cable parted and she was picked up by the huge waves that fall on Loe Bar and dumped on the shingle, breaking her back. The entire crew of 120 was lost. They drowned within a short distance of the shore so that onlookers could hear their cries for help but were powerless to save them. Several local men exasperated by the situation attached ropes to their waists and waded into the surf in an attempt to reach the ship only to be beaten down by the waves and barely escaping with their own lives.

One of the people who witnessed this wreck was a Helston man called Henry Trengrouse. He vowed to find a way to help prevent disasters like the Anson. He invented a rocket apparatus that was fired from the cliff or beach and was able to carry a line aboard the stricken ship. The crew could then be brought ashore by a chair and pulley system. The apparatus saved many hundreds of lives. It is only in the last few years that this system has been withdrawn from service being superseded by rescue helicopters. The helicopters that patrol this part of the coast often pass over the site of the wreck of the Anson on their way to and from their base at Culdrose.

Recommended Walk

Circular walk around Loe Pool

Whilst you can walk around the whole of Loe Pool in a day many people choose to walk smaller sections starting at one of the five car parks dotted around the area. A track follows the busier western side of the pool and this is especially popular with cyclists. The footpath on the eastern side is much quieter.

Distance: 8 km/5 miles round the edge of Loe Pool (4 hrs).
Parking: Car parks are dotted all around the edge of Loe Pool. Going: Easy. Pub/Refreshments: Nothing directly on the route of this walk, but there are pubs and cafes in Porthleven & at Halzephron above Gunwalloe Fishing Cove.
Best time of year to visit: During any storm to watch the huge waves that crash onto Loe Bar. The spring and autumn bring migrating birds to the pool. In the summer look out for the Yellow Horned Poppy on the bar near the pool outlet.

Section 2.
Gunwalloe, Poldhu & Mullion

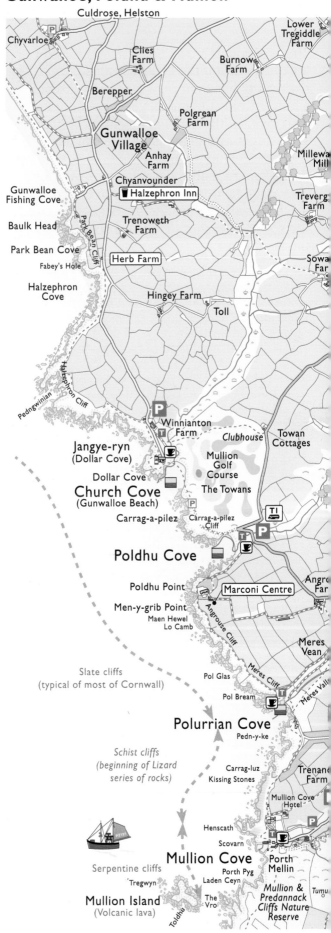

Culdrose, Helston

Chyvarloe

Lower Tregiddle Farm

Clies Farm

Burnow Farm

Berepper

Polgrean Farm

Gunwalloe Village

Anhay Farm

Millewa Mill

Chyanvounder

Halzephron Inn

Gunwalloe Fishing Cove

Treverg Farm

Baulk Head

Trenoweth Farm

Park Bean Cove

Park Bean Cliff

Herb Farm

Fabey's Hole

Sowa Far

Halzephron Cove

Hingey Farm

Toll

Halzephron Cliff

Pedngwinlan

Winnianton Farm

Clubhouse

Towan Cottages

Jangye-ryn (Dollar Cove)

Mullion Golf Course

Dollar Cove

The Towans

Church Cove (Gunwalloe Beach)

Carrag-a-pilez

Carrag-a-pilez Cliff

TI

Poldhu Cove

Poldhu Point

Marconi Centre

Angro Far

Men-y-grib Point

Maen Hewel Lo Camb

Angrouse Cliff

Meres Vean

Slate cliffs (typical of most of Cornwall)

Pol Glas

Meres Cliff

Meres Vall

Pol Bream

Polurrian Cove

Pedn-y-ke

Schist cliffs (beginning of Lizard series of rocks)

Carrag-luz Kissing Stones

Trenan Farm

Mullion Cove Hotel

Henscath

Scovarn

Mullion Cove

Porth Mellin

Serpentine cliffs

Porth Pyg

Laden Ceyn

Mullion & Predannack Cliffs Nature Reserve

Tregwyn

The Vro

Mullion Island (Volcanic lava)

Toldhu

20

This single part of the coast has four of the best beaches on the Lizard Peninsula. Everybody has their personal favourite but Church Cove at Gunwalloe is probably the best loved with its ancient isolated church, sand dunes and legends of lost Spanish treasure in Dollar Cove. Poldhu and Polurrian are within easy reach of Mullion and much favoured by locals. In this area for the first time the slate rocks give way to the schists that start the Lizard sequence of unusual rocks.

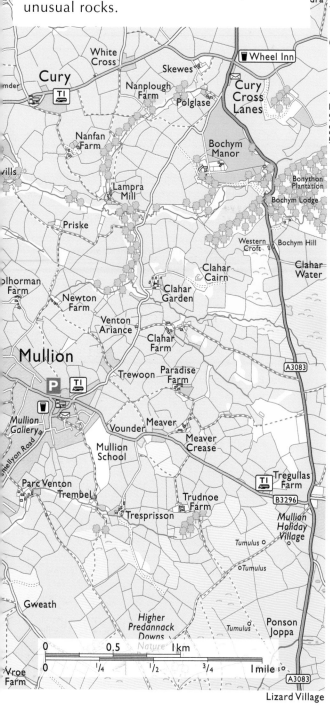

Jangye-ryn (Dollar Cove)
In the contorted strata of the cliffs you can get some feeling for the power of earth movements that result from continental drift. These slates were originally laid down in shallow water as horizontal layers. As the layers built up over many millions of years the pressure of overlying sediment turned the ooze into solid rock. Movements of the earths crustal plates has squeezed them into vertical contorted folds.

Dollar Cove
If the tide and currents are right storms sometimes throw up silver dollars from the wreck a 17th century ship.

Church Cove, Gunwalloe
Wonderful beach in all seasons. The lonely setting of the small church is not unusual in Cornwall where many churches are set in isolated coves away from settlements. In the 6th & 7th centuries a tide of Celtic Christian holy men landed in Cornwall from Wales, Ireland & Brittany to convert the locals. A sacred enclosure would be built on the place where a Celtic saint landed or lived and later a church was constructed.

Mullion
The largest village on the Lizard peninsula and with a good selection of facilities including craft workshops and galleries. It is only a short walk to the coast from Mullion and you can take your pick of some of the best beaches on the whole peninsula.

Mullion Cove & Island
Boat trips leave from the harbour in the summer to view the coastline and watch seals. Mullion Island is formed from the lavas that erupted onto the Rheic sea floor 375 million years ago. They represent the uppermost layers in the ophiolite. The island is a breeding colony for a number of species of seabird. Great black backed gulls breed here as do shags, cormorants, guillemots and kittiwakes.

Marconi and Poldhu
On the cliffs above the south side of Poldhu Cove and beyond the large Victorian building that is Poldhu residential home there is an exhibition and memorial to Guglielmo Marconi. In December 1901 the first radio signal to cross the Atlantic was sent from here to Newfoundland and so started the revolution of radio that changed the world forever. The radio station was the forerunner of our modern digital communications now received and transmitted from Goonhilly Satellite Station.

Section 3.
Predannack & Kynance Cove

In this part of the Lizard coastline the underlying geology and its effect on the landscape are very evident. Predannack Head is a plug of schist rock surrounded by a mass of serpentine. Above Mullion Cove the serpentine forms magnificent brooding cliffs. They are succeeded by the high schist cliffs of Predannack Head in turn only to be trumped by the serpentine of Vellan Head. This part of the coast feels very raw and remote, a feeling intensified by the Stone and Bronze Age burial mounds that are visible on the horizon across the plateau of Goonhilly Downs.

Ogo-dour Cove
This beautiful little bay feels very isolated but is within easy reach of the National Trust car park at Predannack Wollas and it is a good place to picnic. The cove marks the boundary between the schists to the north and serpentine to the south and is common place to spot seals.

Mullion & Predannack Cliffs Nature Reserve
In April the cliffs are covered in a delightful blue haze of spring squill. Also look out for Green Winged Orchids and rare Wild Chives. The National Trust maintain the cliff and heath habitat by grazing wild ponies and Soay sheep to keep down the grasses and increase the diversity of wild plants. It is particularly noticeable how the soil above the schist is well cultivated around Predannack whereas the cliffs above Mullion Cove and south of Ogo-dour Cove are left wild because the infertile serpentine bedrock.

Predannack Airfield
Base for RAF fighter command during the second world war and predates the present naval air station at Culdrose of which this is now a satellite field. It is used for training helicopter pilots and practising helicopter based commando assaults. Fire fighting practice is also carried out on derelict planes. The plumes of smoke are a common sight during the summer.

Recommended Walk
Wild flowers on Mullion & Predannack Cliffs
This is a quiet section of the coast. The two great attractions of this walk are the dramatic cliffs and the rich variety of wildlife to be observed. In the spring the cliffs are sparkling with flowers and if you're lucky you will get a glimpse of a Cornish Chough - a red billed and footed member of the crow family that has started to breed on this coast for the first time in fifty years. In the autumn seals breed in the caves towards Lizard Point and are often visible basking on rocks.

Distance: *5 km/3 miles round trip (2 hours).* *Parking:* *Large car parks at Mullion Cove. Small National Trust car park at Predannack Farm.* *Going:* *Generally OK some steep climbs.* *Pub/Refreshments:* *Cafe at Mullion Cove. Pasties at Mullion Bakery. Pubs in Mullion village.*

Serpentine cliffs

Mullion Village

P

T

Henscath

Scovarn

Mullion Cove

Porth Pyg

Laden Ceyn

Porth Mellin

Tregwyn

The Vro

Recommended Walk

Mullion Island
(Pillow lava)

Toldhu

Mullion & Predannack Cliffs Nature Reserve

Vroe Farm

Wh Uni

Old Quarry

Stone Cross
Early Christian

The Chair

Predannack Morva

Bosvean

Higher Predannack

Maen-te-heul

Teneriffe Farm

Schist cliffs

Pedn Crifton

Predannack Manor

Higher Predannack Wollas Farm

P

Windyridge Far

Predannack Head

Lower Predannack Wollas Farm

Parc Bean Cove

Ogo-dour Cove

Pol Cornick

Velvet Rock

George's Cove

Vellan Head

Pengersick

Gew-graz

Pigeon Ogo

The Horse

Serpentine cliffs

Rill Point

Rill Ledges

Kynance Cove

Immortalised as the perfect cove by romantic painters and poets in the C18th and C19th. Walking down from the car park look out for the purple flowers of Bloody Crane's-bill which cover the cliffs here in the summer. The cliffs to the north of the cove are home to Wild Thyme and the small brown flower spikes of the parasitic Thyme Broomrape that feeds on the roots of the wild thyme. Make sure you arrive when the tide is falling as many of the caves with their beautiful naturally polished walls are inaccessible at high water.

0   0.5   1km

0   1/4   1/2   3/4   1 mile

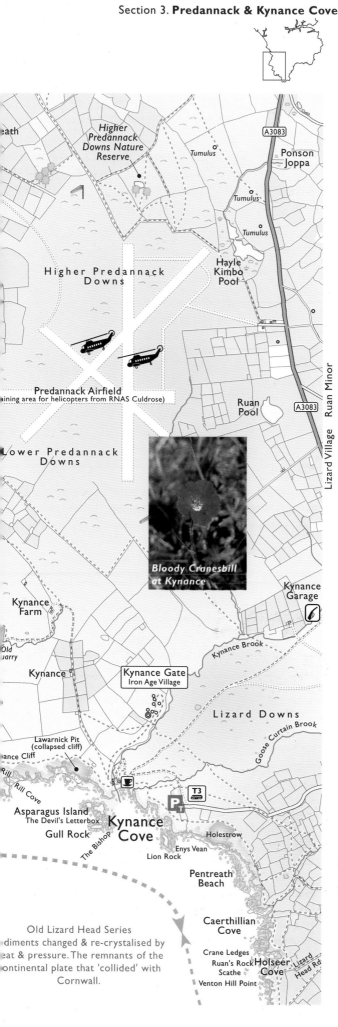

eath

Higher Predannack Downs Nature Reserve

Tumulus

A3083

Ponson Joppa

Higher Predannack Downs

Tumulus

Hayle Kimbo Pool

Tumulus

Predannack Airfield
(training area for helicopters from RNAS Culdrose)

Lower Predannack Downs

Ruan Pool

A3083

Ruan Minor

Lizard Village

Bloody Cranesbill at Kynance

Kynance Garage

Kynance Farm

Kynance Brook

Old Quarry

Kynance

Kynance Gate
Iron Age Village

Lizard Downs

Goose Curtain Brook

Lawarnick Pit
(collapsed cliff)

ance Cliff

Rill

Rill Cove

T3

Asparagus Island
The Devil's Letterbox

Kynance Cove

Holestrow

Gull Rock

The Bishop

Lion Rock

Enys Vean

Pentreath Beach

Caerthillian Cove

Old Lizard Head Series
diments changed & re-crystalised by
eat & pressure. The remnants of the
ontinental plate that 'collided' with
Cornwall.

Crane Ledges
Ruan's Rock
Scathe
Venton Hill Point

Holseer Cove

Lizard Head Rd

Section 4.
Lizard Point, Cadgwith & Kennack Sands

Lizard Point like its western counterpart, Land's End is fully exposed to the south westerly storms that spin and spiral north from the Equator in the autumn and winter. There have been at least 500 documented shipwrecks on the reefs that snake out to sea from Lizard Point. As a consequence even today this small area boasts a lighthouse, a lifeboat station and a coastwatch lookout. At the beginning of this century it used to also boast a radar station, a radio station and a symaphore and telegrapgh station.

Lizard Point

This is the most southerly point in mainland Britain and a perfect place for a late afternoon or evening stroll as the sun sets. Frosts are almost unknown on these cliffs such is the warming influence of the surrounding sea. Rare plants such as the tiny, low growing *Fringed Rupturewort* and the fern, *Sea Spleenwort* thrive locally. The colourful succulent *Hottentot Fig* has escaped from local gardens to colonise the cliffs west of Lizard Point.

The position of Lizard Point as the first landfall for ships arriving from the Atlantic has meant that even from the beginning of historic times the Lizard has been a prominent landmark. The Greeks mention the Lizard as an important landmark on the tin trade route between the Mediterranean and Cornwall. In more recent times it has been a centre of communications with the maritime telegraph station at Bass Point.

The rocks of the reefs off Lizard Point are thought to be the only visible outcrop of the Normannian plate whose collision with 'Cornwall' 375 million years ago caused the Lizard rocks to be thrust from the sea floor to the surface.

Lizard Lighthouse

The present Lizard Lighthouse was erected in 1752 to replace a failed private lighthouse built by the Falmouth privateer Sir John Killigrew in 1619. Sir John thought he could run a good scam by charging passing shipping for the provision of the light. He never made the lighthouse pay and it soon went dark. Sir John and his family always lived on the edge of the law. His wife Lady Jane, was a notorious pirate. She was charged with robbing a ship seeking haven in Falmouth harbour and of murdering two of the crew in the process. Her two accomplices were tried, found guilty and beheaded. Lady Jane was pardoned by the magistrate who by strange coincidence happened to be her husband.

Old Lizard Lifeboat Station

This station was sited here in the days when the lifeboat had to be rowed out to aid ships - this was simply the nearest point to the main wrecking ground. The exposed position of the slip restricted its operation so that in 1962 a new house and slip were built at the more sheltered Kilcobben Cove near Church Cove.

The Hansey, wrecked at Pen Olver, November 1911.

Housel Bay - see photo on front cover

This was the terminal for a pioneer undersea communications cable completed between the Lizard and Bilbao in Spain in 1872. The cable terminated at Lizard Signal Station on the cliff above. The cable was only in operation for four years before the terminal was moved to the more sheltered sandy beach at Kennack Sands because of repeated damage sustained in heavy weather on the rocky seabed of Housel Bay. The original cable is still clearly visible cut into the cliff face.

Bass Point

The Lizard Signal Station on Bass Point was constructed in 1872 by the shipping agents Fox and Company of Falmouth (the owners of Glendurgan garden on the Helford) so that cargo laden ships inbound from the Atlantic could communicate by semaphore flag with the station. The ship owner could then be telegraphed and could relay orders to the captain as to which markets were giving the best prices. When they arrived at Lizard Point ships may have been at sea for months without communication with their owners. The captain would then be instructed to either sail up the west coast to Bristol and Liverpool, or up the English Channel to London and the continental ports. In 1883 the operation was taken over by Lloyds of London. The red painted wall by the footpath is a daymark and aligns with the building behind and Balk daymark above Church Cove to help ships establish the position of Vrogue Rock.

Church Cove

Landewednack church is dedicated to St Winwaloe of Landevennec in Brittany (and Gunwalloe in Section 2) an area closely associated with Cornwall. There is a small cafe in the old pilchard palace above the cove.

Cadgwith

Cadgwith is the quintessential Lizard village - self reliant and resilient. The thatched roofs of the houses in the cove are testament to the battering Cadgwith can get in the winter. The roofs are held down by chains weighted with boulders. The local pub is known throughout West Cornwall for the singing of Cornish songs on a Friday night. Just south of the village is the Devil's Frying Pan - a massive hollow in the cliffs resulting from the collapse of a sequence of caves.

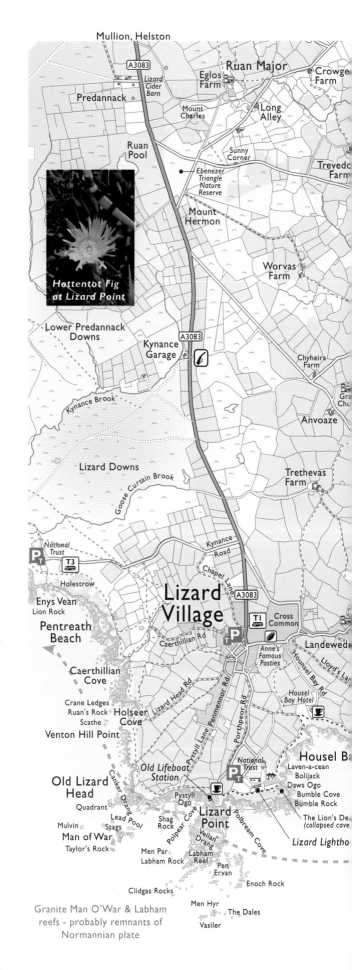

Mullion, Helston

A3083

Ruan Major

Crowge Farm

Eglos Farm

Lizard Cider Barn

Predannack

Mount Charles

Long Alley

Ruan Pool

Sunny Corner

Trevedo Farm

Ebenezer Triangle Nature Reserve

Mount Hermon

Worvas Farm

Hottentot Fig at Lizard Point

Lower Predannack Downs

A3083

Kynance Garage

Chyheira Farm

Anvoaze

Kynance Brook

Lizard Downs

Goose Curtain Brook

Trethevas Farm

Kynance Road

National Trust

T3

Holestrow

Chapel Lane

A3083

Lizard Village

Enys Vean

Lion Rock

Pentreath Beach

Cross Common

Landewedn

Caerthillian Rd

Anne's Famous Pasties

Lloyd's La

Housel Bay Rd

Caerthillian Cove

Housel Bay Hotel

Lizard Head Rd

Crane Ledges
Ruan's Rock
Scathe

Holseer Cove

Venton Hill Point

Housel B

National Trust

Housel B

Laven-a-cean
Bolijack
Daws Ogo
Bumble Cove
Bumble Rock

Old Lifeboat Station

Old Lizard Head

Quadrant

Pystyll Lane

Penmennor Rd

Porthpeor Rd

The Lion's De.
(collapsed cave

Pystyll Ogo

Lizard Point

Polbream Cove

Lizard Lightho

Mulvin

Lead Pool
Stags

Shag Rock

Man of War

Taylor's Rock

Canker Drang Pool

Polpear Cove

Vellan Drang

Labham Rock

Men Par

Labham Reef

Pen Ervan

Enoch Rock

Clidgas Rocks

Men Hyr

The Dales

Granite Man O'War & Labham
reefs - probably remnants of
Normannian plate

Vasiler

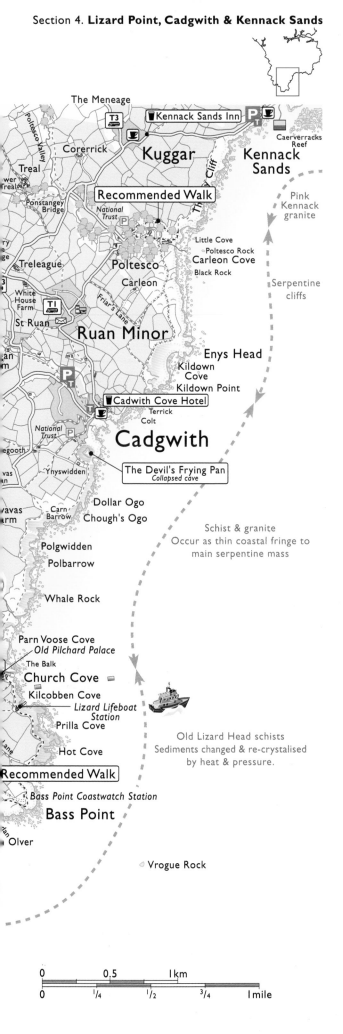

The Meneage

Kennack Sands Inn

Caerverracks Reef

Corerrick

Kuggar

Kennack Sands

Treal

wer Treal

Ponstangey Bridge

Pink Kennack granite

Recommended Walk

National Trust

Treleague

Poltesco

Little Cove

Poltesco Rock

Carleon Cove

Black Rock

Serpentine cliffs

Carleon

White House Farm

St Ruan

Ruan Minor

Enys Head

Kildown Cove

Kildown Point

Cadgwith Cove Hotel

Terrick

Colt

National Trust

Cadgwith

The Devil's Frying Pan
Collapsed cave

Ynyswidden

Dollar Ogo

Carn Barrow

Chough's Ogo

Schist & granite
Occur as thin coastal fringe to
main serpentine mass

Polgwidden

Polbarrow

Whale Rock

Parn Voose Cove
Old Pilchard Palace

The Balk

Church Cove

Kilcobben Cove

Lizard Lifeboat Station

Prilla Cove

Old Lizard Head schists
Sediments changed & re-crystalised
by heat & pressure.

Hot Cove

Recommended Walk

Bass Point Coastwatch Station

Bass Point

Olver

Vrogue Rock

0   0.5   1 km

0   1/4   1/2   3/4   1 mile

Kennack Sands

Kennack Sands is one of those magical places where childhood memories are forged. It is a combination of classic geological site and fantastically good beach. The wide, sandy foreshore has an unrivalled selection of beautiful pebbles from the different rocks that are exposed in the surrounding cliffs. The predominant rock is the pink Kennack granite that occurs in relatively small outcrops throughout the whole of the southern part of the Lizard. It is always deeply weathered and decomposed forming pockets of good soil on the otherwise uncultivated serpentine soils. Its relative weakness compared with the serpentine means that it forms the broad valleys behind Kennack Sands and Cadgwith. These valleys provide shelter against the winds that whip across the exposed plateau of Lizard Downs in the winter. Just below where the road reaches the beach there are a number of different rocks cutting across each other. It is this sequence that helped to establish the relative ages of some of the rocks in of the Lizard.

Recommended Walk
Circular walk from Lizard village to Church Cove

This popular walk starts from the car park in Lizard village or from the National Trust car park above Lizard Point. Best to take pasty and eat at one of the many benches overlooking the sea. When the tide is out, Housel Bay makes a good place to stop and swim.

Distance: 4.5 km/3 miles. *Parking:* Large car parks at Lizard village, Lizard Point - small car park at Church Cove. *Going:* Moderate. *Pub/Refreshments:* Cafe & pubs in Lizard village or pick up a pasty from 'Anne's Famous Pasty Shop'. Teas and bar snacks available all year from the Housel Bay Hotel. Seasonal cafes at Lizard Point and Church Cove.

Recommended Walk
The serpentine workshops at Poltesco

This is a pleasant stroll down to the sea from the National trust car park. The walk can be easily extended to Kennack Sands to the north or south to Cadgwith.

Distance: 1 km/0.75 mile. *Parking:* National Trust car park at Poltesco. *Going:* Easy. *Pub/Refreshments:* Nearest shop at Ruan Minor. Cafe and pub at Cadgwith, pub at Kuggar.

Shipwrecks around the Lizard

The Suevic on the Men Hyr, Lizard Point 1907.

The Lizard has been prominent in the history of shipping from ancient times by virtue of its position on the main trading routes to and from the Atlantic. Sometimes joyously greeted as a welcome landfall after a long sea voyage, but all too often grimly surveyed by seamen as their graveyard as helpless sail ships were driven before a storm onto the rocks. It is difficult now to appreciate the loss of life a storm could bring. Severe storms would commonly lead to the loss of hundreds of lives at sea.

The whole coast of the Lizard Peninsula is hazardous. Reefs such as The Stags, Man O'War and the Manacles lie low in the water at high tide waiting to take any ship that ventures too close. Whilst it is undoubtedly true that the people of Cornwall often welcomed a wreck as an opportunity to salvage valuable cargo it is not true that ships where commonly lead onto the rocks by false lights. In fact it probably was not necessary given the carnage a prolonged storm or gale would inflict on shipping.

It was only with the advent of the camera at the end of the 19th century that we get graphic evidence of the cost. Many of the most horrific wrecks occurred in poorly maintained and overcrowded ships and before the establishment of an effective lifeboat service. Even when the early lifeboats were introduced they were simply sturdy rowing boats and were as powerless against a storm as any other ship. It must have taken extraordinary courage for the first lifeboatmen to put to sea in a storm with only cussed determination and raw muscle power to fight the sea.

In many cases the victims of shipwrecks were buried on the cliff top above where they were found. This practice arose because it was impossible to tell which victims were Christians, and therefore whether they had a right to a burial in consecrated ground. More practically, no churchyard could accommodate the terrible loss of life that could result even from a single wreck. For instance, the 120 victims of the *Anson* lost on Loe Bar in 1807 were interned above the bar. The 200 victims of the *Royal Anne* wrecked in 1720 on the Man O'War reef, were buried in Pistol Meadow near Lizard Point.

Being wrecked does not always end in disaster though. In 1882, the *Mosel* bound for America with emigrants hit Bass Point in thick fog. Such was the way she lay that the passengers and crew where able to walk ashore on to the cliffs as if they were disembarking at a port. The *Suevic* ran onto the Men Hyr in thick fog in 1907. The Lizard, Cadgwith, Coverack & Porthleven lifeboats rescued 456 of the 524 passengers & crew. The wreck was blown in half and the stern section towed back to Southampton where a new bow was attached.

Section 5.
Coverack, St Keverne & The Manacles

Coverack

This area of the Lizard sits on gabbro bedrock. The coast is studded by numerous small deserted quarries blasted into the cliff face and by two huge working quarries. The gabbro is quarried to make aggregate for roads and for rock armour to protect vulnerable coasts in other parts of the south west. It produces extremely willing soils making this one of the most fertile farming districts in Cornwall. The rich soils in this part of the Lizard have been cultivated from prehistoric times.

Coverack

Coverack was built on the success of pilchard fishing in the 19th century and although the pilchard shoals have long since disappeared a number of small boats still carry on the maritime tradition by working the inshore waters. A lifeboat was stationed here until 1963 primarily because of the danger of ships striking the Manacles. The name of the local pub, *The Paris Hotel* recalls the wreck of the *Paris* on the Manacles. Some of the ship was salvaged and now forms part of the hotel. On a summer evening you can sit outside the Paris Hotel and gaze across Coverack Bay to the Manacles as they emerge above a falling tide.

St Keverne

St Keverne is the main settlement and centre of the farming community on the east coast of the Lizard. The gabbro and schist soils of this area form rich and productive soils. The combination of mild winters and being in the sheltered lee of Goonhilly Downs ensure that there is a long and productive growing season here. This gives local farmers the opportunity to get their crops to market two or three weeks ahead of their competitors further north in Britain. They can therefore charge a premium price for their produce.

Late Stone Age (4,000-2,500BC) pottery has been found in the crevices of Crane Carrick Crags and the local gabbro clay was used to make pottery that has been found all over England - evidence of a surprisingly wide web of prehistoric trade and commerce. The area around Lowland Point is rich in prehistoric field boundaries and the remains of prehistoric huts.

In more recent times the area acquired a reputation for some serious smuggling. The infamous Long Meadow Gang operated from Godrevy Cove in the 18th century. The church has a memorial to the victims of the *Mohegan* wrecked on the Manacles in 1898. Just south of the village is Tregellast Barton the home of Roskilly's Ice Cream. There are craft shops, a restaurant and you can see the process of making ice cream. A trail follows the stream down the valley past wildlife pools.

The Manacles

These rocks are particularly dangerous as they are almost submerged at high water. In the times before the invention of radar, ships would often navigate by hugging the coastline. As a consequence, the Manacles have claimed almost as many victims as Lizard Point.

The Bay of Panama

Porthkerris

Serves as a base for divers working on the Manacles reef and gives tuition for novices. Cafe/restaurant above the beach during the summer. The cliff to the north has been quarried away to form a platform just above sea level. The MOD observation post was constructed to observe test firing of torpedoes.

Porthallow

Fishing has always been important to Porthallow. Small inshore boats work from the beach catching lobsters and crabs on the reefs and ledges around this part of the coast. The boats are hauled up onto the beach by winch when not in use and during the winter when the seas are too rough. Pilchards were the main stay of the fishing industry until the pilchard shoals disappeared almost overnight at the beginning of this century due to over fishing. A courtyard fish cellar or pilchard palace has been converted into a cafe on the south side of the beach. It was here that the fish were stacked and pressed to extract water and oil before being packed into barrels for export to the Catholic countries of southern Europe. The fish were popular because of the tradition of not eating red meat on Fridays and at Lent.

The Five Pilchards pub has some of the wreckage recovered from the *Bay of Panama* which went aground on Nare Head in the Great Blizzard of March 1891. The ship was homeward bound from Calcutta for Dundee with a cargo of jute fibre for use in making sacks and door mats. When the ship hit the rocks some of the crew climbed the masts where they became frozen solid to the rigging. The captain, his wife and six crew were lost. The survivors were cared for locally, and then sent off to Falmouth by road so that they could join ships to their home ports. Unfortunately, the storm was not completely blown out and the small party and their horses were caught in another blizzard, barely escaping with their lives again after they became trapped in snow drifts.

The Helford River & The Meneage

The Helford remains the most unspoiled of the rivers of Cornwall. Ancient oak forests cover most of the river banks and the deep sheltered valleys allow subtropical plants to flourish, protected from frost by the warming influence of the surrounding sea. World renowned plant collections are open to the public at Glendurgan and Trebah near Helford Passage. The modern car and road network find the river a hindrance but for most of the past 3,000 years it is the river that has been the major route of communication. Indeed the best way to explore the area around the Helford is to see the river not as a barrier but as a way into the landscape. There can be no better way to pass a day than to hire a boat and take a picnic up the river exploring the wooded creeks that are so characteristic of the Helford and stopping at one of the many small quays that dot the river banks.

The northern and the southern banks of the river have differing characters. The southern bank, known as The Meneage (Cornish for *Land of the Monks*) has remained first and foremost a rural agricultural area. Its relative inaccessibility to modern transport protecting it from development and giving it a feeling of isolation and separateness. The north bank has a long industrial history associated with the granite rock of the Carnmenellis granite boss that makes up the high ground to the north. The quays at Port Navas were built to serve the granite quarries and the moors above Constantine are covered with haunting, deserted quarries and old mine workings.

As well as providing building stone the granite also holds tin and copper ore and tin has been carried on the river for at least 2,000 years from the time of the Celtic

Right. Prehistoric standing stone at Mawgan. Left. The hamlet of Durgan on the north bank of the Helford River. Glendurgan Garden runs up the valley behind the houses.

Iron Age (600BC-AD43) to the end of nineteenth century. The importance of the Helford as a tin trading route in the Iron Age is illustrated by the defensive promontory and hill forts that occupy almost every bend in the river. The forts are usually constructed of a circular ditch and bank such as at Gear and Caervallack, near Mawgan. They all occupy strong defensive sites, and were perhaps used as places of refuge in periods of conflict as well as permanent settlements or courts for local chieftains. The Iron Age fort at Dennis Head near St Anthony was reused during the English Civil War to protect the tin trade. Even Trelowarren House sits within ancient earth works.

The Iron Age peoples also built the mysterious underground passages called fogous - from the Cornish word ogo for cave. An especially good example is Halliggye Fogou at Trelowarren House (Section 6). This is the best example of a fogou in the whole of Cornwall. It has a number of side passages and portals. Despite investigations by archaeologists there is no clear explanation of their function. Suggested functions vary from the purely practical such as a food store to the religious and sacred.

The Romans never settled this far south west in Britain, but they certainly traded tin here even before they invaded Britain in AD43. When they retreated 400 years later to defend their homeland against Barbarian and Vandal attacks, Britain sunk into a dark age. The Christian religion that Emperor Constantine had brought to Britain also died away, only surviving in the monastic and hermitical traditions of Wales and Ireland. During the 6th and 7th centuries these wild Celtic men and women travelled

A 2,738 ton block of granite from Polkannuggo Quarry near Mabe on the north bank of the Helford. This is claimed to be the largest single block of granite ever quarried.

from their remote homes to reestablish Christianity among their Celtic brothers and sisters in Cornwall and Brittany. This period is known in Cornwall as the Coming of the Saints. They created a synthesis of the older Celtic pagan tradition and Christianity. Hence many churches such as St Anthony are found in isolated sites near springs or overlooking the sea, a reflection of the Celtic tradition of nature worship and they are usually dedicated to obscure Cornish saints. Mawnan Church is actually built within the boundaries of an Iron Age fort. A very clear message to the population that the church now possessed the authority and power associated with the ancient site. In the following centuries these missionaries became the Celtic Saints of Cornwall.

The Cornishman in the 17th and 18th century was a Jack of all Trades - he needed to be with a large family and meagre wages. He would have cultivated a small holding, fished and worked in the mine or quarry when work was available. When the wars with France caused the Crown to levy steep taxes on the few affordable luxuries, such as tobacco, wine and brandy, the Cornishman exercised his right to free trade. Of course what was free trading to a Cornishman was smuggling to an Excise Man.

At this time communication and transport was almost completely confined to the sea. The Cornishman probably had more in common with his Breton cousins with whom he shared a Celtic language and culture, than with the English. It was therefore natural that free trading should flourish despite the heavy penalties for being convicted. There was a ready market and large profits to be made for a smuggler. Local gentry were certainly involved as were many of the customs men themselves, often turning a blind eye in return for a healthy commission.

The trade was so well accepted that some pubs became known as The Wink from the custom of winking at the Landlord to let him know that you wanted the real French brandy that he kept out of the way under the counter rather than the legal. The geography of this part of the Cornish coast might have been specially designed for smuggling with its numerous tiny, hidden coves and beaches. Customs officers based in Falmouth were simply unable to cover the multitude of small inlets and coves. Daphne Du Maurier's famous novel Frenchman's Creek, set on the Helford, creates a vivid picture of this period of history.

Section 6.
Gweek, Goonhilly & Trelowarren

There is a delightful contrast in this section between the windswept downs of Goonhilly with its satellite dishes and the sheltered velvety creeks of the Helford river. The upper reaches of the Helford are particularly quiet and serene. They are cloaked in ancient oak woods that reach to the waters edge. The river is only accessible at two places in this section. Firstly, at Tremayne Quay near Trelowarren House and secondly, at Frenchman's Creek near Helford village and both are worth a visit.

Gweek

This little village was in past centuries the hub of a large industrial and commercial operation. Even today the quays on the south bank are used by the international sea engineering company Seacore. Gweek first grew in importance because of its role as the port for Helston when Helston's original harbour on the River Cober became blocked by the growth of Loe Bar in early medieval times. The lucrative trade of exporting copper and tin from the mines north of Helston in the 18th and 19th centuries gave Gweek an importance beyond its modest size. The port went into decline at the end of the 19th century when the tin price crashed and the mines closed. The last great sail ships that docked in Gweek were to carry away miners and their families in the great emigration that followed the decline of the mines. Gweek is home to the National Seal Sanctuary.

Goonhilly Downs & Earth Satellite Station

Goonhilly Downs are the mysterious dark heart of the Lizard and a defining landscape on the peninsula with its wide open skies and unusual habitats. The rare *Cornish Heath* thrives here and is frequently to be seen draped with lethargic sun bathing adders. The serpentine bedrock produces such poor soils that this area has been uncultivated by man since he first arrived here 10,000 years ago. It is an extremely rare example of almost virgin habitat. Instead man has populated the downs with burial mounds of Stone and Bronze Age kings and standing stones such as Dry Tree menhir (see back cover). Dry Tree is the highest part of the downs and was formerly the site of public hangings. It is said - mostly in pubs late at night - that the ghosts of highwaymen hanged at Dry Tree still haunt the moors preying on any person foolish enough to venture across the downs at night.

The Earth Satellite Station continues the long tradition of communications installations on the Lizard. Pioneered by the maritime telegraph station at Bass Point and the transatlantic radio station at Poldhu. The Earth Satellite Station was established in the early 1960's and is now the busiest and largest satellite station on earth relaying millions of telephone call, TV links and internet services every day. Tours of the site are available during the season and there is a visitor exhibition with plenty of hands on exhibits for children and dads.

Constantine

Gweek
Gweek Inn

Bonallack

National
Seal
Sanctuary

Bonallack
Wood

Ponsontuel
Creek

Culdrose, Helston

Ponson
Tuel

Australia

Mawgan Creek

Bishop
Quay

Gwarth-an-drea

Bridge
Farm

Halanowet
Farm

Mawgan
Cross

Gear
Bridge

Celtic Cross

Mawgan
Bridge

Gear
Farm

T2/3

Old Count House

Trelowarren
Mill

Mawgan

Culdrose, Helston

CarleenVenton
Gannal

Itching
Post

Ten
Brid

Entrance to
Trelowarren
House →

Pond Lodge

The Lizard
Countryside Ce

Garras

Halliggy Fogou
(Iron Age underground passage)

The
Mount

P

Lower
Garras
Farm

Halliggye
Farm

Trelowarr
House

Tregear

Gilly Farm

Chybilly

Kaledna

B3293

Chygarkye

Chygarkye

Bojorrow

The

Tregadjack

Skyburriowe

Trevassack

T2

Burnoon

Trevassack
Quarry
(serpentine)

Cury Cross Lanes, Mullion

Goonhilly

Tregaddra

Goonhilly Earth Station
& Visitor Centre

Higher
Tregaddra

Bonython Manor

0   0.5   1km

0   ¼   ½   ¾   1mile

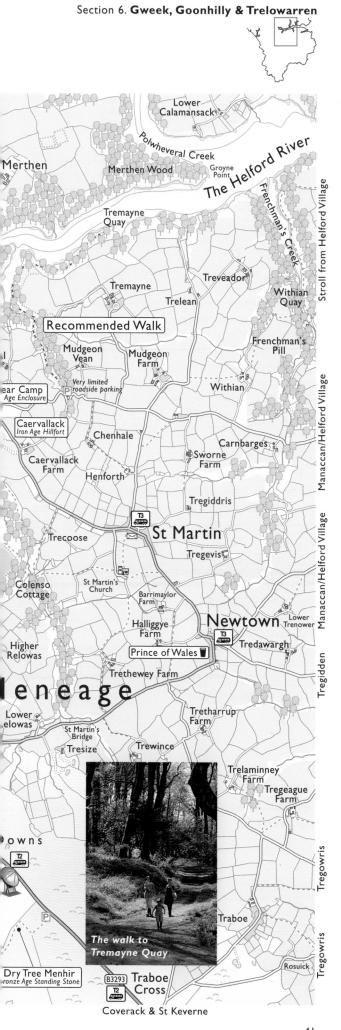

Lower Calamansack

Polwheveral Creek

Groyne Point

The Helford River

Merthen

Merthen Wood

Frenchman's Creek

Tremayne Quay

Stroll from Helford Village

Treveador

Withian Quay

Tremayne

Trelean

Frenchman's Pill

Recommended Walk

Mudgeon Vean

Mudgeon Farm

Withian

ear Camp
Age Enclosure

Very limited roadside parking

P

Caervallack
Iron Age Hillfort

Chenhale

Carnbarges

Manaccan/Helford Village

Caervallack Farm

Henforth

Sworne Farm

Tregiddris

T3

Trecoose

St Martin

Tregevis

Manaccan/Helford Village

Colenso Cottage

St Martin's Church

Barrimaylor Farm

Newtown

Lower Trenower

Higher Relowas

Halliggye Farm

Prince of Wales

Tredawargh

Tregidden

Ieneage

Trethewey Farm

Lower elowas

St Martin's Bridge

Tresize

Trewince

Tretharrup Farm

Trelaminney Farm

Tregeague Farm

owns

T2

Traboe

Tregowris

P

The walk to Tremayne Quay

Rosuick

Dry Tree Menhir
ronze Age Standing Stone

B3293

Traboe Cross

T2

Tregowris

Coverack & St Keverne

Trelowarren & The Lizard Countryside Centre

Trelowarren is the ancestral home of the Vyvyan family. The stables and outhouses have been converted to provide accommodation for a bistro, pottery, and craft centre and for The Lizard Countryside Centre. Walks meander through the woods and a path links up with the delightful stroll down to Tremayne Quay on the Helford River.

Halliggye Fogou

Fogous are underground chambers or passages and Trelowarren boasts the best example in Cornwall. The function of a fogou is uncertain as archaeological remains have only rarely been found within them. They are generally associated with Iron Age (700BC- 410AD) settlements such as Chysauster and Carn Euny near Penzance. The settlement associated with this fogou is now lost to view but one of the underground passages opens into the ditch that once surrounded the settlement. It is thought that they functioned as cool, underground stores for food but some ceremonial or religious function cannot be ignored because of their relatively complex and large scale construction. Another popular explanation is that they may have been hidden refuges if the settlement was under attack.

Tremayne Quay

This walk is a continuation of the woodland walk from Trelowarren House, but unlike the woodland walk this riverside walk is open all year. There is only enough space for two cars to park on the roadside. During the summer it is probably easiest to park at Trelowarren House. The land is now owned by the National Trust but used to belong to Trelowarren Estate.

Tremayne Quay and the well made drive was built for a royal visit of Queen Victoria. The walk follows the wooded valley to the edge of the river, then through open fields, finally passing through oak woods to the quay. Take a picnic and swim from the quay. On the opposite bank is Merthen Wood an ancient wood coppice for charcoal to fuel tin blowing houses, lime kilns and harvested of bark to tan cow hides.

Recommended Walk
A walk to Tremayne Quay

This walk follows the driveway that once linked Trelowarren House to Tremayne Quay on the Helford River. The quay has views over to the wooded north bank of the Helford and has plenty of room for a picnic. Parking is very restricted at the roadside but during the tourist season you could park at Trelowarren and make this a continuation of the woodland walk around the grounds

Distance: *3 km/2 miles round trip (2 hours).* **Going:** *Easy.*
Car Parking: *Room for just 2 cars at the roadside.*
Pub/Refreshments: *Restaurant and bar at Trelowarren House, pubs at Gweek, Mawgan, Newtown & Manaccan.*

Section 7.
St Anthony, Manaccan & Helford

The landscape of this part of the Meneage has both a gentle timeless and a conspiratorial atmosphere. The steep wooded valleys and narrow lanes come as something of a relief after the relentless, exposed downs of Goonhilly. But don't be misled by the quietness of the river today - this river has seen plenty of adventure. Firstly as a haven to smugglers and pirates in the C18th and more recently as a base for secret agents of the SOE during the Second World War. The creeks are best explored by boat from the river.

Glendurgan Garden

The garden was started by the Fox family. They were Quaker merchants and shipping agents at the large port of Falmouth which became prosperous as a Royal Mail packet station in the C18th and C19th. Mail and parcels from all over the world were landed at Falmouth to be taken on to their destination by road. The Fox family paid sea captains to bring back seeds and specimen plants from all over the world for their collection. The gardens are at their best in the spring when the camellias are in flower. The garden is particularly well known for its collection of rare and exotic trees and the large Laurel Maze which has recently been restored. At the bottom of the valley is the little hamlet of Durgan, built as an utopian village with a tiny school for local children. The garden is owned by the National Trust.

Trebah Garden

A sub tropical ravine garden. A stream winds through water gardens with waterfalls and ponds stocked with Koi carp to Polgwidden Cove on the Helford. The garden is particularly famed for its collection of 100 year old Australian tree ferns and its rhododendrons and magnolias Another plant that thrives in the sheltered moist, mild climate is the giant rhubarb *Gunnera manicata*. The leaves of which are so large they can be used as an umbrella There are lots of children's trails and a secret play area. Visitors to Trebah are also able to use the private beach at Polgwidden Cove for picnics and swimming.

Polgwidden Cove

The concrete roadway that winds down the valley side was built during the Second World War to allow access to the beach for tanks and armoured personnel carriers embarking onto landing craft for D-Day. The US 29th Infantry Division embarked here for the assault on Omaha Beach in Normandy. They had the misfortune to land on a beach facing a battle hardened division of German troops recently transferred from the Russian front. As a consequence they received 83% casualties in the first three hours. This part of the river was also used by the Special Operations Executive (SOE) to spirit agents in and out of occupied France using in a French trawler and also to mount missions to pick up allied aircrew sheltered by the Resistance.

Falmo

The Red Lion

Mawnan Smith

Lower Penpoll

Durgan
Crossroads

Trewince

Trenarth
Bridge

Narrow Road

Bos

Port
Navas

T4

P

Pons-a-verryn

Trebah
Crossroads

Glendurgan
Garden

Port Navas Creek

P

Bosl

Quay

Budock
Vean Hotel

Trebah
Wartha

P

Golf Course

Trebah
Garden

Durgan

Greb
Beac

Pill
Cove

Perran
Cove

Helford
Passage

Durgan
Beach

Calamansack
Wood

T4

P
T

Robin's Cove

Polgwidden
Cove

Ferry Boat Inn

Passage
Cove

Padgagarrack Cove

Bosahan Co

Pedestrian Ferry
(summer)

Penarvon
Cove

Helford Pt

Permissive path through
Bosahan Estate
No dogs or cycling

Shipwrights Arms

Treath

P
T

Bosahan
House

Bosahan
Garden

T3

P

Roadside
2 cars

Helford
Village

Condur

Bosahan
Barton

Underwood

Recommended Walk

Kestle

Frenchman's
Pill

Halvose

Roscaddon

Trudgwell

Penpoll
Mill

Gillar

Carne

Tregith

Carne Creek

Manaccan

P

The New Inn

T3

Tregonwell

Tregonwell
Mill

Lanarth

Tregithew

Landrivick
Farm

Choon

Trelowry

The Meneag

Crowns

Trezebel

Trevaddra

Higher
Boden

Rosl
Ba

Treworgie Mill

Higher
Trenower

House at Carne Creek.

Barvansack

Tregidden

Tregidden
Farm

Polpridnick

Lesneague

0   0.5   1km

0   1/4   1/2   3/4   1mile

Traboe

St Kev

Constantine/Gweek/Helston

Walk to Frenchman's Creek

St Martin

Newtown

Newtown

Traboe

The Helford River

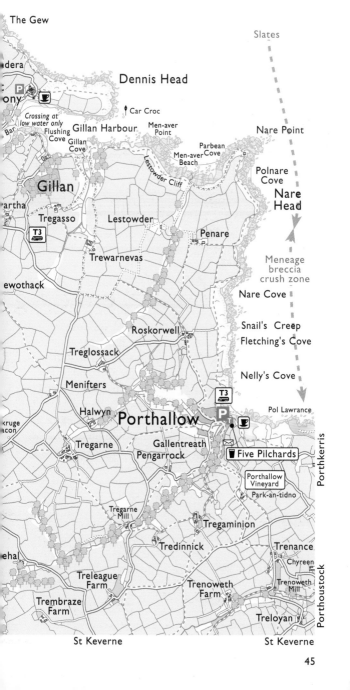

Helford Village

This sleepy little place was a prominent port in past centuries. The creek is lined with small quays hinting at the busy trade once carried through the port. In the early medieval period Cornwall and Brittany shared a common Celtic language and culture. This was at a time when family links with Celtic cousins in Brittany where as strong as those with that other foreign country, England. The custom house at Helford village was intended to collect tax from imported goods such as French rum, tobacco and lace. When trade with France was banned because of the Napoleonic Wars the river became instead became a haven for 'free traders' or pirates. A pedestrian ferry links the north and south banks of the river. It runs from Helford village to Helford Passage and allows you to walk to the gardens at Glendurgan and Trebah on the north bank. There are also a number of good beaches on the north bank side of the river, the best being Grebe beach as well as the isolated sandy beaches near Bosahan.

Manaccan

Manaccan is perfectly placed to act as a base for exploring the banks of Carne Creek to Helford village and Frenchman's Creek. Starting from Manaccan avoids the necessity of driving into Helford village which is often very busy in the summer. There is a fine thatched pub - the *New Inn* with a beer garden that is perfect for children. The beautiful church has a Fig tree growing from the wall of the tower. Local superstition insists that the tree should not be harmed or it will bring bad luck to the village.

Recommended Walk

A circular walk to Rosemullion Head
(via pedestrian ferry from Helford village)

The pedestrian ferry from Helford village runs all summer except at low water on a spring tide. Once on the north side of the Helford you are within walking distance of the sub tropical gardens at Trebah and Glendurgan. Alternatively, you might just walk around to Rosemullion Head, explore the rock pools at Nansidwell Cove and have lunch at the *Red Lion* in Mawnan Smith. Returning down Carwinion Valley or along the road to Helford Passage past the valley gardens of Trebah and Glendurgan. The best places to swim is the lovely pebbly beach at Grebe or at Polgwidden Cove (for visitors to Trebah Garden only). Boat hire for exploring the creeks and quays of the river is available from the Helford Passage. You can gain access to Glendurgan & Trebah from the footpath above Durgan or by following the road up from Helford Passage.

Distance: Round trip to Rosemullion Head - 9km/4 miles round trip (3 hours). **Going:** *Good.* **Bus:** *The T4 runs via Helston/Helford Passage/Mawnan Smith & Falmouth.* **Car Parking:** *Car parks at Helford village, Helford Passage & Mawnan Church. National Trust car park above Grebe Beach.* **Pub/Refreshments:** *Cafes at Glendurgan & Trebah Gardens. Pubs- Shipwrights Arms at Helford Village, Ferry Boat Inn at Helford Passage, Red Lion at Mawnan Smith.*

St Anthony & Dennis Head

St Anthony is a tiny tranquil hamlet grouped around the church. The adjacent Dennis Head has fine views across the mouth of the Helford river and Falmouth Bay. The defensive qualities of Dennis Head are immediately apparent; it commands the approaches to the river and has an easily defensible narrow neck on its landward side. The first earthwork defenses are thought to be Iron Age although it was fortified repeatedly over the centuries. Notably in response to the threat of invasion from the Spanish Armada and later on from Napoleon. During the English Civil War the headland was held for the King and was used to protect the vital revenue earning tin trade which funded the Royalist cause. Unfortunately, almost all of the remaining earth works and fortifications are covered by a dense covering of gorse and bracken during the summer but there is at least a wonderful view from the Head across the mouth of the river. Sail and motor boat hire is available from the shop above the beach.

Helford Passage

Passage Cove with the *Ferry Boat Inn* (known locally as the F.B.I.) sitting at the top of the beach make this an enjoyable place for families to visit. There plenty of rock pools to explore at low water. Boats are available for hire to explore further up the river and for land lubbers that are good walks all the way towards the mouth of the Helford including rope swings for children to climb near Cow beach.

Recommended Walk

A circular stroll to Frenchman's Creek

Frenchman's Creek is famously the setting for the novel by Daphne DuMaurier and is one of the loveliest walks in the area taking in wooded valleys and creeks. The walk is at its best early in the morning or in the evening. You can start from Helford Village or if that is very busy start from Manaccan. From Helford Village take the sign posted path from the head of Helford Creek up the wooded valley. Follow the path to Kestle Farm, cross the road and follow the track down the hill to Frenchman's Creek. Just before the head of the creek a path leaves on the right and follows the bank towards the river To return to Helford follow the path as it climbs up the hill. It joins a track and then the public road. The road runs down the hill to Penarvon Cove and Helford. A more direct route to Helford Village is to turn right along the road, walk 50 metres where a track called Orchard Lane runs down the hill on the left back to the village.

Distance: *3.5 km/2 miles round trip (1.5 hours).* **Going:** *Good - steep climb out of Penarvon Cove/Helford village.*
Bus: *The T3 runs between Helston, Helford Village, Manaccan & St Keverne.* **Car Parking:** *Large car park at Helford Village, roadside parking at Manaccan, room for 2 cars to park at the end of the road past Kestle.*
Pub/Refreshments: *Cafe at Helford village. Shipwrights Arms at Helford Village of New Inn at Manaccan.*

Some Common Cliff Plants

Thrift (left)
Also known as the cliff rose. Note the lichens and samphire in the background.

Sea campion (above). One of the first Spring flowers to appear on the cliffs often in large dense mats.

Sea Carrot (left)
A very characteristic plant of exposed cliffs. The most perfect examples have a single purple flower at their centre. Often found dwarfed by the hostile conditions. The candied roots where once sold as an aphrodisiac.

Yarrow (above)
Usually found with very bright, intense white flowers and feathery leafs but this pink variety is also common. About 30cm tall.

Bell Heather (left)
Common on both the downs and the cliffs. Often found in prostrate form growing close to the ground for protection from the wind.

Lousewort (left)
Like many members of the figwort family Lousewort is a hemi-parasite. Supplementing its own food production by taking nutrients from the roots of its host - usually heather. About 7cm tall.

Gorse (above)
One the dominant shrubs on both the coastal heath and moorland. The flowers give it away as member of the pea family. Sometimes found covered with the pink parasitic threads of dodder. Flowers all year but at its best in April when on still sunny days the heady coconut perfume from the flowers can be quite overpowering.

Spring Squill (left)
forms a misty carpet across the cliffs in early spring at Lizard Point and Mullion Cliff. It is often mistaken for a dwarfed variety of bluebell - both are members of the lily family. A very uncommon variety flowers in the autumn.

PICTURE CREDITS
Paul Watts - front cover, pp4, 33, 36;
Frank Gibson - pp19, 27, 31;
Andrew Besley - p24;
Royal Institution of Cornwall - pp35, 38;
all other photos Neil Reid
Published by Cormorant Design
PENZANCE Cornwall
Telephone (01736) 369194
First published 1999.
This edition published 2003.
© Neil Reid 2003
ISBN 0-9520874-3-X

Kidney Vetch (above)
Sometimes known as Bacon and Eggs because of its colouring.